CANVA FOR STUDENTS: MASTERING DESIGN FOR SCHOOL PROJECTS AND BEYOND

Er. Avinash Singh

Table of Contents:

- Introduction to Canva
- Getting Started with Canva
- Basic Design Principles
- Creating Your First Design
- Advanced Design Techniques
- Collaborating on Canva
- Canva for Presentations
- Canva for Social Media
- Canva for Posters and Flyers
- Canva for School Reports and Essays
- Customizing Templates
- Using Canva on Mobile Devices
- Printing and Sharing Your Designs
- Time-Saving Tips and Tricks
- Becoming a Canva Pro

Detailed Book Introduction:

In the digital age, visual content has become a cornerstone of effective communication. For students, mastering the art of design can significantly enhance the quality of their school projects, presentations, and overall academic work. "Canva for Students: Mastering Design for School Projects and Beyond" is a comprehensive guide that aims to empower students with the skills needed to create stunning visual content using Canva, a versatile and user-friendly graphic design tool.

Canva has revolutionized the way we approach design by making it accessible to everyone, regardless of their experience level. Whether you're a high school student preparing a presentation, a college student working on a group project, or simply someone interested in enhancing your design skills, this book is tailored to meet your needs. Our goal is to take you from a novice to a proficient Canva user, capable of producing professional-quality designs with ease.

This book is structured to provide a step-by-step learning experience. We begin with an introduction to Canva, exploring its features, interface, and the variety of tools it offers. You'll learn how to navigate the platform, understand the different types of projects you can create, and get comfortable with the basic functions.

From there, we delve into the foundational principles of design. Understanding these principles is crucial as they form the backbone of any good design. We cover concepts such as color theory, typography, layout, and composition. With this knowledge, you'll be able to make informed design choices that enhance the visual appeal and effectiveness of your projects.

Once you have a solid grasp of the basics, we guide you through the process of creating your first design. This hands-on approach helps reinforce what you've learned and gives you practical experience using Canva's tools. You'll be creating everything from simple graphics to more complex designs, learning advanced techniques along the way.

Collaboration is an integral part of modern education and work environments. Canva's collaboration features make it easy for multiple users to work on a project simultaneously, providing feedback and making adjustments in real-time. We dedicate a chapter to exploring these features, ensuring you can efficiently collaborate with classmates and teachers.

Presentations are a significant part of student life, and Canva excels in this area. We show you how to create engaging and visually appealing presentations that will captivate your audience and enhance your communication. Similarly, social media has become a key platform for sharing information and ideas. In this book, you'll learn how to create compelling social media graphics that stand out in a crowded digital landscape.

The versatility of Canva extends to other formats like posters, flyers, school reports, and essays. We provide detailed instructions and tips for designing these documents, ensuring they are not only informative but also visually impressive. Customizing templates is another powerful feature of Canva that we cover in detail, allowing you to personalize your designs to fit your specific needs.

With the increasing use of mobile devices, we also explore how to use Canva's mobile app to create and edit designs on the go. This flexibility ensures you can work on your projects anytime, anywhere. Additionally, we discuss the various options for printing and sharing your designs, whether you need physical copies or digital files.

To help you work more efficiently, we share a range of time-saving tips and tricks. These insights will help you streamline your workflow and make the most of Canva's features. Finally, for those looking to take their skills to the next level, we provide guidance on becoming a Canva Pro, unlocking advanced features and capabilities.

"Canva for Students: Mastering Design for School Projects and Beyond" is your ultimate resource for becoming proficient in Canva. By the end of this book, you'll have the confidence and skills to create outstanding designs that will impress your teachers, peers, and anyone who views your work. Let's embark on this creative journey together and unlock your full potential with Canva.

Chapter 1: Introduction to Canva

Canva is a powerful online design tool that has transformed the way people create graphics, presentations, and other visual content. Founded in 2012 by Melanie Perkins, Cliff Obrecht, and Cameron Adams, Canva aims to democratize design by providing an easy-to-use platform accessible to everyone, regardless of their design experience.

What is Canva?

At its core, Canva is a web-based graphic design tool that offers a wide range of features and tools to help users create professional-quality designs. Canva's intuitive drag-and-drop interface allows users to create stunning visuals by combining text, images, and other design elements. With thousands of templates, fonts, and graphics available, Canva caters to a diverse set of design needs, from social media posts and marketing materials to presentations and educational resources.

The Importance of Visual Content

In today's digital age, visual content is more important than ever. Studies have shown that people are more likely to engage with and remember information presented visually. For students, this means that well-designed visuals can enhance learning, improve retention, and make their work stand out. Whether it's a presentation, a report, or a social media post, effective visual design can significantly impact the way information is perceived and understood.

Why Canva for Students?

Canva is particularly beneficial for students for several reasons:

1. **User-Friendly Interface:** Canva's simple and intuitive interface makes it easy for students of all ages to start creating designs without any prior experience.
2. **Variety of Templates:** Canva offers a vast library of templates specifically designed for educational purposes, including presentations, posters, infographics, and more.
3. **Collaboration Features:** Canva allows multiple users to collaborate on a single project in real-time, making it perfect for group assignments and projects.
4. **Accessibility:** Canva is available online and as a mobile app, enabling students to work on their designs from anywhere, at any time.

Getting Started with Canva

To begin using Canva, you'll need to create an account. Here's a step-by-step guide to get you started:

Canva
Design spotlight
Business
Education
Plans and pricing
Log in
Sign up

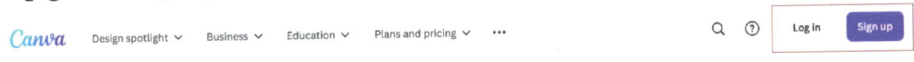

1. **Sign Up:** Go to Canva's website (www.canva.com) and sign up using your email address, Google account, or Facebook account.

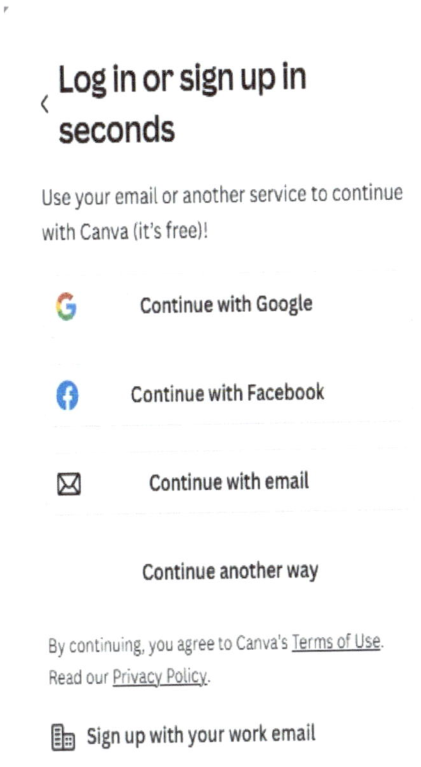

Log in or sign up in seconds
Use your email or another service to continue with Canva (it's free)!
Continue with Google
Continue with Facebook
Continue with email
Continue another way
By continuing, you agree to Canva's Terms of Use. Read our Privacy Policy.
Sign up with your work email

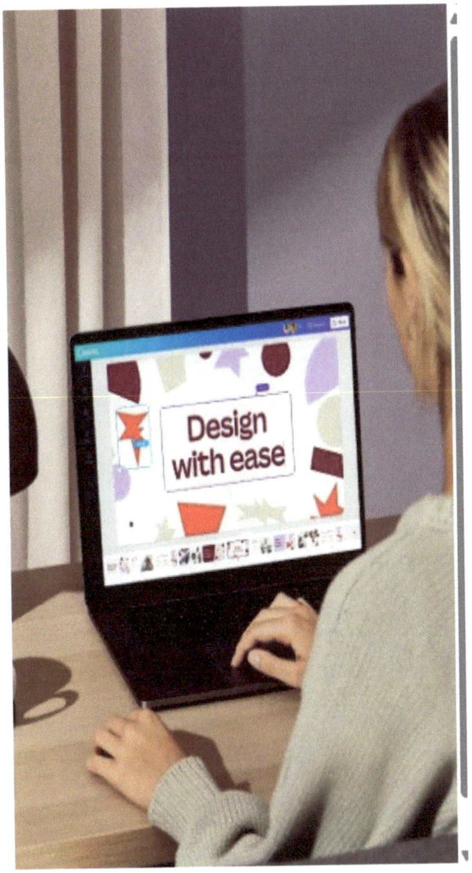

Design with ease

2. **Choose Your Account Type:** Select the "Education" option if you're a student or teacher. This will give you access to Canva's educational templates and resources.

What will you be using Canva for?

We'll use this to recommend designs and templates especially for you.

Non-profit or Charity
You're here to design for the greater good

Teacher
You're here to empower your students

Personal
You're here to make anything and everything

Large company
You're here to scale your brand and keep it consistent

Small Business
You're here to design your brand from the ground up

Student
You're here to impress your teachers and classmates

‹ **Where are you currently studying?**

We have thousands of templates on Canva for various schools and subjects, we will show you the most relevant ones.

○ University

○ Professional development

○ High School

○ Vocational training, trade school, or other

Continue

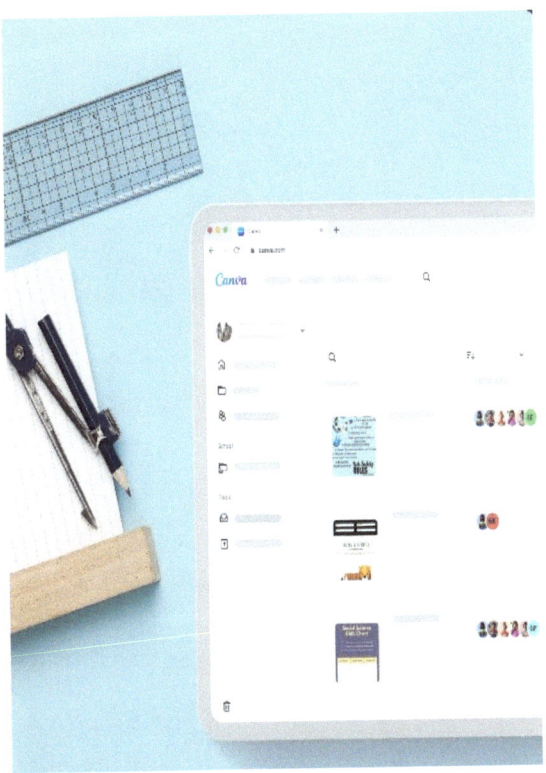

‹ **Enjoy the best stuff for free with Canva for Education**

If your school is already with Canva for Education, you can use our premium features for free!

👑 Use our coolest features like **Magic Resize, Background Remover**, and **premium animations**

🎁 **100 million+ premium photos, videos and elements**, 3000+ premium fonts and 610,000+ premium templates

🎓 Collaborate with your friends and classmates in any kind of Canva design

Unlock Canva for Education

3. **Explore the Dashboard:** Once you've created your account, you'll be taken to the Canva dashboard. Here, you can start

9

a new design, explore templates, and access your saved projects.

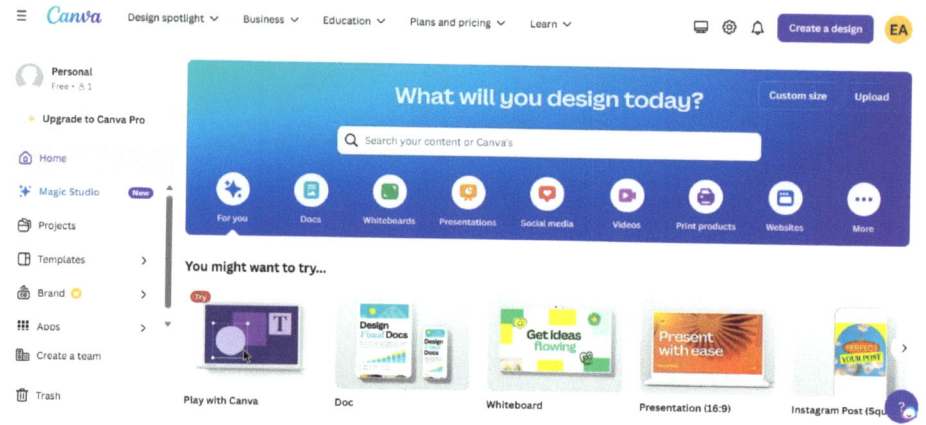

Exploring Canva's Features

Canva offers a wide range of features designed to help you create professional-quality designs. Some of the key features include:

1. **Templates:** Canva's extensive library of templates covers various categories, such as social media, presentations, posters, and more. Templates are a great starting point for your designs and can be customized to fit your needs.

2. **Elements:** Canva provides a vast collection of design elements, including photos, illustrations, icons, and shapes. These elements can be added to your designs and customized as needed.

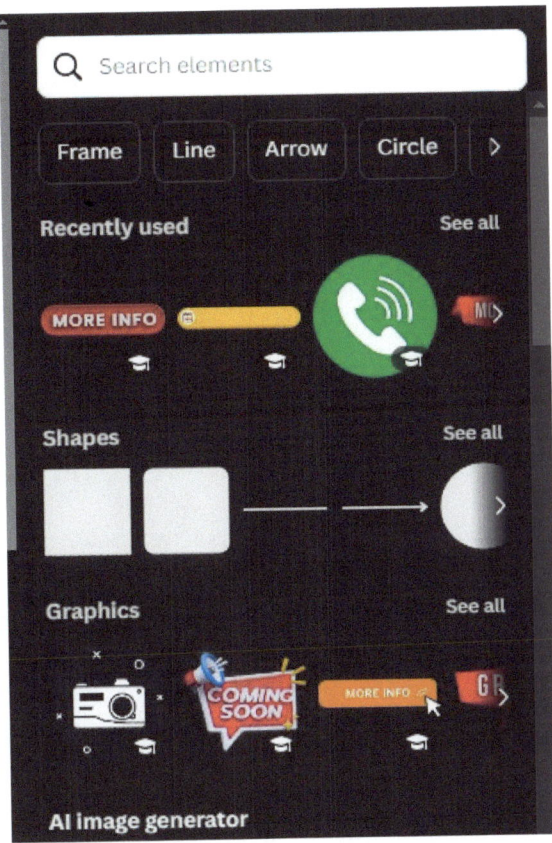

3. **Text Tools:** Canva offers a variety of fonts and text formatting options to help you create visually appealing typography. You can adjust the size, color, alignment, and spacing of your text to achieve the desired effect.

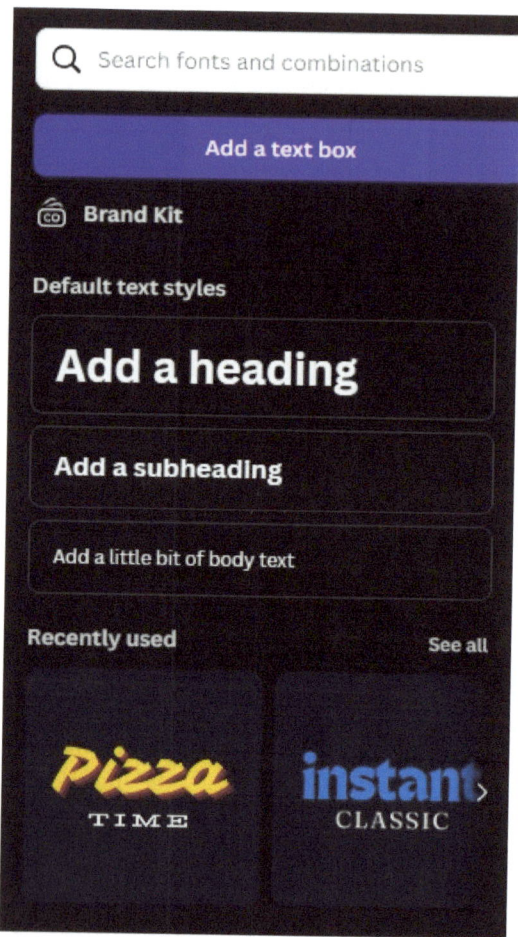

4. **Backgrounds:** Canva allows you to choose from a wide range
    of backgrounds, including solid colors, gradients, patterns,
    and images. Backgrounds can add depth and interest to your
    designs.

5. **Uploads:** Canva lets you upload your own images and graphics, giving you complete creative control over your designs. You can also access your uploads from any device by logging into your Canva account.

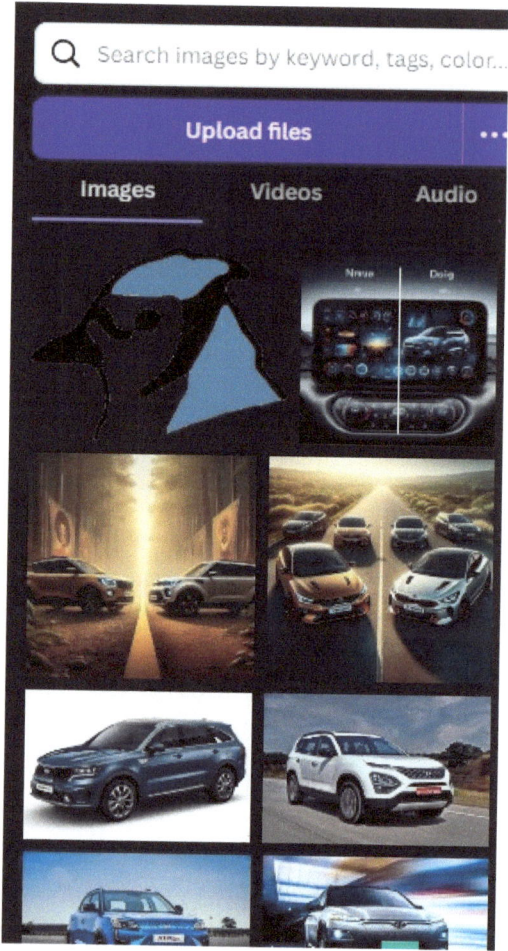

6. **Collaboration:** Canva's collaboration features enable multiple users to work on a project simultaneously. You can share your designs with others, leave comments, and make real-time edits.

Canva for Education

Canva offers special features and resources for educational users, making it an invaluable tool for students and teachers alike. Some of the educational features include:

1. **Classroom Kits:** Canva provides classroom kits with templates and resources tailored for teachers and students. These kits cover a wide range of subjects and can be used to create lesson plans, assignments, and more.
2. **Educational Templates:** Canva's library includes templates

specifically designed for educational purposes, such as worksheets, flashcards, and certificates. These templates can save time and help students create polished and professional-looking projects.

3. **Student Collaboration:** Canva allows students to collaborate on group projects, making it easy to work together and share ideas. Teachers can also use Canva to assign group projects and provide feedback in real-time.

In the next chapters, we will dive deeper into the various aspects of using Canva for your school projects and beyond. From mastering basic design principles to exploring advanced techniques, this book will equip you with the skills needed to create impressive and effective visual content. Let's get started on this exciting journey of creativity and learning with Canva!

Chapter 2: Getting Started with Canva

Creating a Canva account is the first step toward unlocking the full potential of this versatile design tool. In this chapter, we'll guide you through the process of setting up your account, navigating the Canva interface, and exploring the various tools and features available to you.

1. Creating Your Canva Account
2. **Visit Canva's Website:** Go to www.canva.com.
3. **Sign Up:** Click on the "Sign up" button. You can sign up using your email address, Google account, or Facebook account.

Log in or sign up in seconds

Use your email or another service to continue with Canva (it's free)!

G   Continue with Google

f   Continue with Facebook

✉   Continue with email

      Continue another way

By continuing, you agree to Canva's Terms of Use. Read our Privacy Policy.

▤ Sign up with your work email

4. **Select Your Account Type:** Choose the "Education" option if you're a student or teacher. This will give you access to Canva's educational templates and resources.
5. **Complete Your Profile:** Fill in your details and set up your profile. This will help personalize your Canva experience and

make it easier to find relevant templates and resources.
6. Navigating the Canva Interface

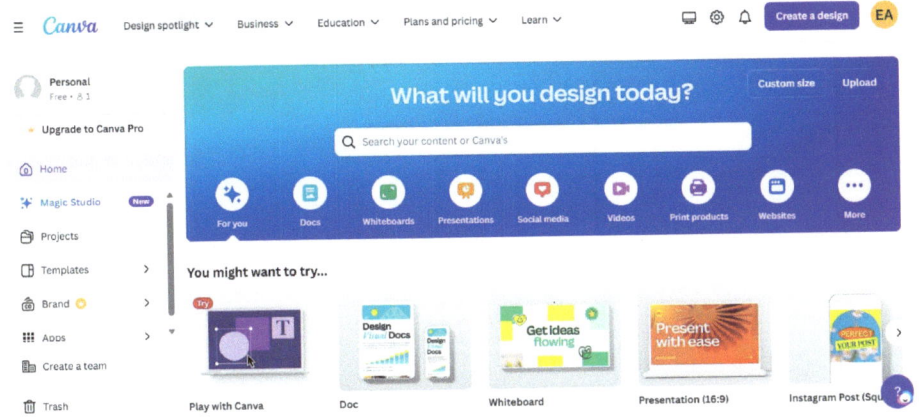

Once you've created your account and logged in, you'll be taken to the Canva dashboard. Here's an overview of the main sections and features you'll find:

1. **Home:** This is your main landing page where you can start a new design, access your saved projects, and explore templates.
2. **Templates:** Browse Canva's extensive library of templates organized by category, such as social media, presentations, posters, and more.
3. **Projects:** Access your saved designs and folders where you can organize your work.
4. **Brand Kit:** For users with a Canva Pro account, the Brand Kit allows you to save brand colors, fonts, and logos for easy access.
5. **Design Tools:** The design tools are located on the left-hand side of the editor screen. These include elements, text, backgrounds, and uploads.
6. Invite others to collaborate on your design by sharing a link or adding their email address.

Starting Your First Design

Creating your first design in Canva is a straightforward process. Follow these steps to get started:

1. **Choose a Template:** From the dashboard, click on "Create a design" and select the type of project you want to create, such

17

as a presentation, poster, or social media post.

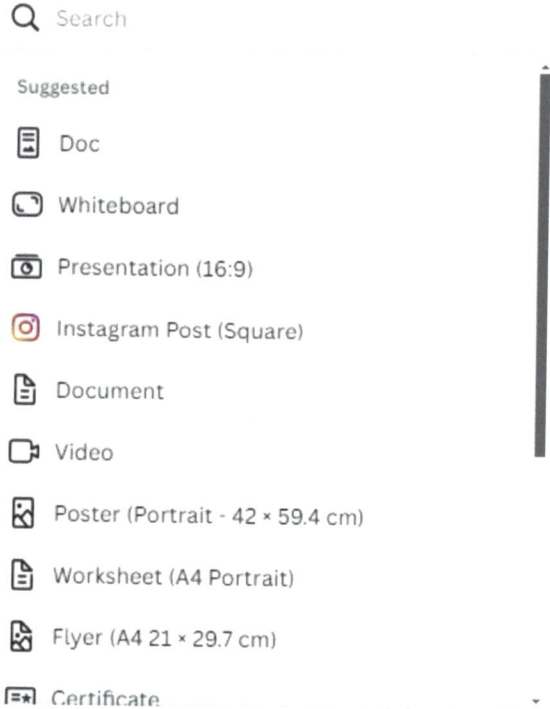

2. **Customize the Template:** Once you've selected a template, you can start customizing it to fit your needs. Use the design tools on the left-hand side to add elements, text, backgrounds, and images.
3. **Save Your Design:** Canva automatically saves your work as you go. However, you can also manually save your design by clicking on the "File" menu and selecting "Save."
4. **Download or Share:** Once you're happy with your design, you can download it as a file or share it directly from Canva. Click on the "Download" button to choose your preferred file format, or use the "Share" button to send a link to your design.

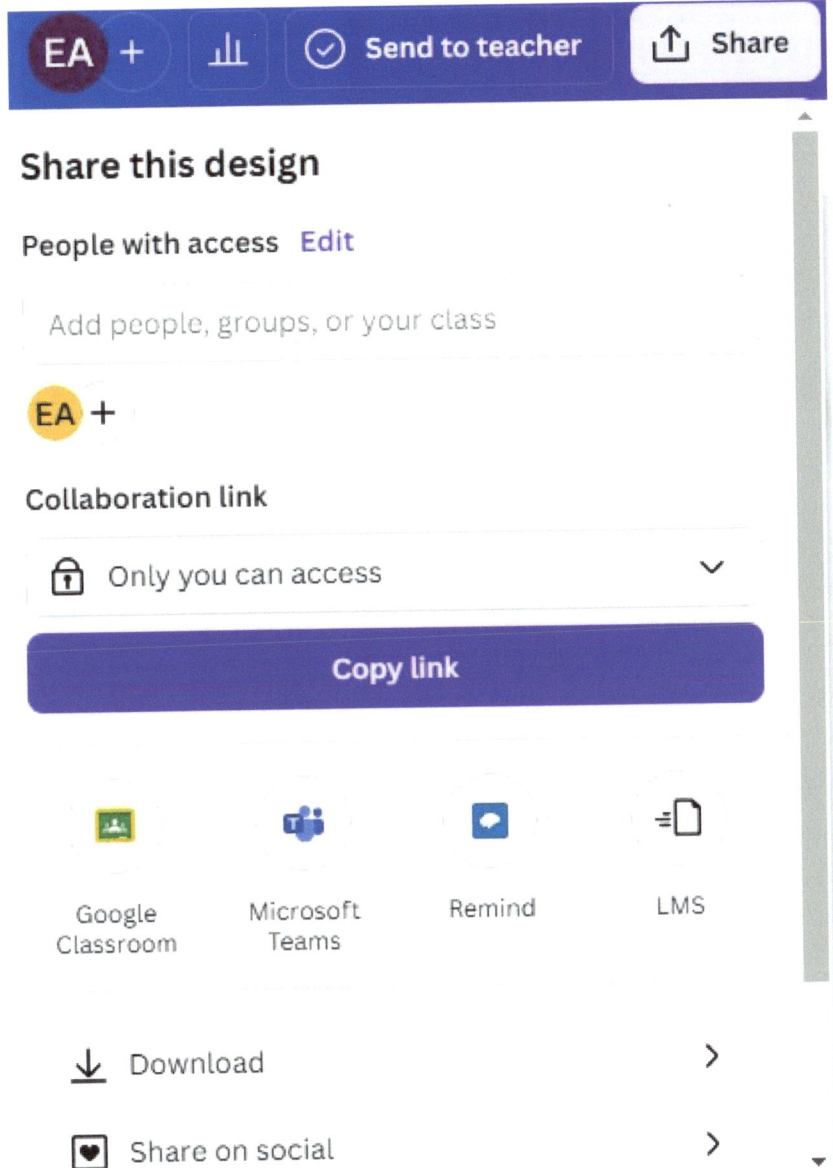

Exploring Canva's Tools and Features

Canva offers a wide range of tools and features to help you create stunning designs. Here's a closer look at some of the key tools you'll be using:

1. **Elements:** Canva provides a vast collection of design

elements, including photos, illustrations, icons, and shapes. These elements can be added to your designs and customized as needed.

2. **Text Tools:** Canva offers a variety of fonts and text formatting options to help you create visually appealing typography. You can adjust the size, color, alignment, and spacing of your text to achieve the desired effect.

3. **Backgrounds:** Canva allows you to choose from a wide range of backgrounds, including solid colors, gradients, patterns, and images. Backgrounds can add depth and interest to your designs.

4. **Uploads:** Canva lets you upload your own images and graphics, giving you complete creative control over your designs. You can also access your uploads from any device by logging into your Canva account.

5. **Templates:** Canva's extensive library of templates covers various categories, such as social media, presentations, posters, and more. Templates are a great starting point for your designs and can be customized to fit your needs.

6. **Collaboration:** Canva's collaboration features enable multiple users to work on a project simultaneously. You can share your designs with others, leave comments, and make real-time edits.

Tips for Using Canva

To make the most of Canva's features, here are some tips to keep in mind:

1. **Explore the Templates:** Canva's templates are a great starting point for your designs. Don't be afraid to experiment with different templates and customize them to fit your needs.

2. **Use the Grid and Rulers:** Canva's grid and ruler tools can help you align your elements and create balanced designs. Turn them on by clicking on the "File" menu and selecting "Show grid" or "Show rulers."

Some Important Shortcuts of Canva
- Undo: **Ctrl + Z**
- Redo: **Ctrl + Y**
- Save: **Ctrl + S**
- Select all: **Ctrl + A**
- Add text: **T**
- Add rectangle: **R**
- Add line: **L**
- Add circle: **C**
- Add link: **Ctrl + K**
- Add emoji (Canva Docs and comments only): **Shift + ;**
- Add empty page: **Ctrl + Enter**
- Delete empty page: **Ctrl + Backspace**
- Navigate to toolbar **Ctrl + F1**
- Skip to canvas: **Ctrl + F2**

3. **Take Advantage of Keyboard Shortcuts:** Canva offers a range of keyboard shortcuts to help you work more efficiently. For example, use the "T" key to add text, the "L" key to add a line, and the "R" key to add a rectangle.

4. **Save Your Brand Elements:** If you frequently use the same colors, fonts, or logos, consider saving them in the Brand Kit (available with a Canva Pro account). This will make it easier to access and apply your brand elements to your designs.

5. **Experiment with Effects:** Canva offers various effects and filters that can enhance your designs. Try applying effects like shadows, glows, or blurs to make your elements stand out.

By following these steps and tips, you'll be well on your way to creating stunning designs with Canva. In the next chapter, we'll delve into the basic design principles that will help you create visually appealing and effective designs. Let's continue our journey and unlock the full potential of Canva for your school projects and beyond!

Chapter 3: Basic Design Principles

Design is both an art and a science, requiring an understanding of fundamental principles that guide the creation of visually appealing and effective compositions. In this chapter, we'll explore the key design principles that will serve as the foundation for your work in Canva.

Understanding Design Principles

Design principles are the rules and guidelines that help designers create visually harmonious and functional layouts. These principles include balance, contrast, emphasis, movement, pattern, repetition, proportion, rhythm, variety, and unity. By applying these principles, you can ensure your designs are aesthetically pleasing and communicate your intended message effectively.

Balance

Balance refers to the distribution of visual elements in a design. It can be symmetrical or asymmetrical. Symmetrical balance involves arranging elements evenly around a central axis, creating a sense of stability and order. Asymmetrical balance, on the other hand, uses different elements of varying weights and sizes to create a dynamic and interesting composition. Both types of balance can be used to achieve different visual effects and guide the viewer's eye through the design.

Contrast

Contrast involves using opposing elements, such as colors, shapes, and sizes, to create visual interest and draw attention to key areas of the design. High contrast can make elements stand out, while low contrast can create a more subtle and harmonious look. Effective use of contrast can help emphasize important information and improve the readability of your design.

Emphasis

Emphasis is the process of highlighting the most important elements in a design to make them stand out. This can be achieved through the use of color, size, placement, and other visual techniques. By creating a focal point, you can guide the viewer's attention to the most critical parts of your design.

Movement

Movement refers to the way a viewer's eye is guided through a design. By strategically placing elements and using lines, shapes, and colors, you can create a sense of flow and direct the viewer's gaze from one part of the design to another. Effective use of movement can enhance the storytelling aspect of your design and keep the viewer engaged.

Pattern and Repetition

Pattern and repetition involve using repeating elements, such as shapes, lines, and colors, to create a sense of consistency and cohesion. Repetition can unify different parts of a design and make it more visually appealing. Patterns can also add texture and depth to your design.

Proportion

Proportion refers to the relative size and scale of elements within a design. Proper use of proportion ensures that elements are sized appropriately in relation to each other, creating a balanced and harmonious composition. Proportion can also be used to create emphasis and guide the viewer's eye through the design.

Rhythm

Rhythm is the repetition of visual elements in a design to create a sense of movement and flow. It can be achieved through the use of patterns, lines, shapes, and colors. Rhythm helps establish a visual beat and can make a design more dynamic and engaging.

Variety

Variety involves using different elements and techniques to create visual interest and prevent a design from becoming monotonous. By incorporating a mix of colors, shapes, textures, and sizes, you can add complexity and depth to your design. However, it's important to strike a balance between variety and unity to maintain a cohesive look.

Unity

Unity refers to the overall cohesiveness and harmony of a design.

It ensures that all elements work together to create a unified and consistent visual message. Unity can be achieved through the use of consistent colors, fonts, and styles, as well as the careful placement of elements.

Applying Design Principles in Canva

Now that you understand the basic design principles, let's explore how to apply them in Canva:

1. **Balance:** Use Canva's alignment tools and grids to create symmetrical or asymmetrical balance in your designs. Experiment with the placement of elements to achieve the desired effect.
2. **Contrast:** Choose contrasting colors, fonts, and shapes to make important elements stand out. Canva's color palette and font options make it easy to create high-contrast designs.
3. **Emphasis:** Use size, color, and placement to highlight key elements in your design. Canva's text and element tools allow you to easily adjust these properties to create emphasis.
4. **Movement:** Create a sense of flow by strategically placing elements and using lines and shapes to guide the viewer's eye. Canva's design tools enable you to experiment with different layouts and compositions.
5. **Pattern and Repetition:** Use repeating elements, such as shapes, lines, and colors, to create a cohesive and visually appealing design. Canva's library of elements and patterns can help you achieve this.
6. **Proportion:** Ensure that elements are sized appropriately in relation to each other. Canva's resizing and scaling tools make it easy to adjust the proportion of elements in your design.
7. **Rhythm:** Incorporate repeating elements to create a sense of rhythm and movement. Canva's pattern and alignment tools can help you establish a visual beat.
8. **Variety:** Add visual interest by using a mix of colors, shapes, textures, and sizes. Canva's extensive library of design elements provides endless possibilities for creating variety.
9. **Unity:** Maintain a consistent look and feel by using the same colors, fonts, and styles throughout your design. Canva's brand kit feature can help you achieve unity in your designs.

By applying these design principles, you'll be able to create visually appealing and effective designs that communicate your message clearly and engage your audience. In the next chapter, we'll guide you through the process of creating your first design in Canva, putting these principles into practice. Let's continue our journey and unlock your creative potential with Canva!

Chapter 4: Creating Your First Design

Creating your first design in Canva is an exciting and rewarding experience. This chapter will walk you through the process step-by-step, from selecting a template to customizing your design and adding finishing touches.

Step 1: Selecting a Template

Templates are a great starting point for your designs as they provide a pre-made structure that you can customize to fit your needs. Here's how to select a template:

1. **Go to the Canva Dashboard:** Log in to your Canva account and navigate to the dashboard.

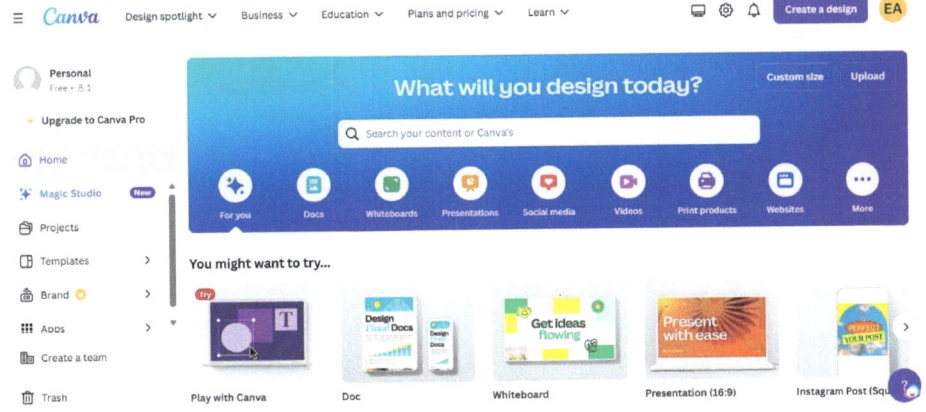

2. **Choose Your Design Type:** Click on the "Create a design" button and select the type of project you want to create. This could be a presentation, poster, social media post, etc.

3. **Browse Templates:** Browse through the available templates. You can filter templates by category, style, or theme to find one that suits your project.

4. **Select a Template:** Once you find a template you like, click on it to open it in the Canva editor.

Step 2: Customizing the Template

Now that you have selected a template, it's time to make it your own. Here are the key elements you can customize:

1. **Text:** Click on any text box to edit its content. You can change the font, size, color, alignment, and spacing using the text toolbar at the top of the editor. Make sure your text is clear and easy to read.

2. **Images:** Replace template images with your own or choose from Canva's extensive library. To upload your own images, click on the "Uploads" tab on the left-hand side and drag your images into the editor. To use Canva's images, click on the "Photos" tab and search for the desired image.

3. **Colors:** Change the colors in your design to match your theme or brand. Click on any element to access the color picker and choose your preferred color. You can also create custom color palettes using the color wheel.

4. **Elements:** Add new elements or replace existing ones. Click on the "Elements" tab to explore shapes, icons, illustrations, and more. Drag and drop elements into your design and resize or reposition them as needed.

5. **Background:** Change the background of your design by clicking on the "Background" tab. Choose from solid colors, gradients, patterns, or images. You can also upload your own background images.

Step 3: Adding Finishing Touches

Once you have customized the main elements of your design, it's time to add the finishing touches:

1. **Alignment and Spacing:** Use Canva's alignment tools to ensure your elements are properly aligned and spaced. This helps create a clean and balanced design.

2. **Effects and Filters:** Apply effects and filters to enhance your images and elements. Click on an image or element, then choose from options like shadows, glows, blurs, and more.

3. **Text Effects:** Add text effects like shadows, outlines, or highlights to make your text stand out. Click on the "Effects" button in the text toolbar to explore the options.

4. **Consistency:** Ensure that your design elements are consistent. Use the same fonts, colors, and styles

throughout your design to maintain a cohesive look.

5. **Review:** Take a step back and review your design as a whole. Make sure everything is aligned, readable, and visually appealing. Ask for feedback from peers or teachers if possible.

Step 4: Saving and Exporting Your Design

Once you're satisfied with your design, it's time to save and export it:

1. **Save:** Canva automatically saves your work as you go, but you can also manually save your design by clicking on the "File" menu and selecting "Save."

2. **Download:** To export your design, click on the "Download" button at the top right corner of the editor. Choose your preferred file format (PNG, JPEG, PDF, etc.) and click "Download."

3. **Share:** If you want to share your design directly from Canva, click on the "Share" button. You can send a link to your design, invite others to collaborate, or post it directly to social media.

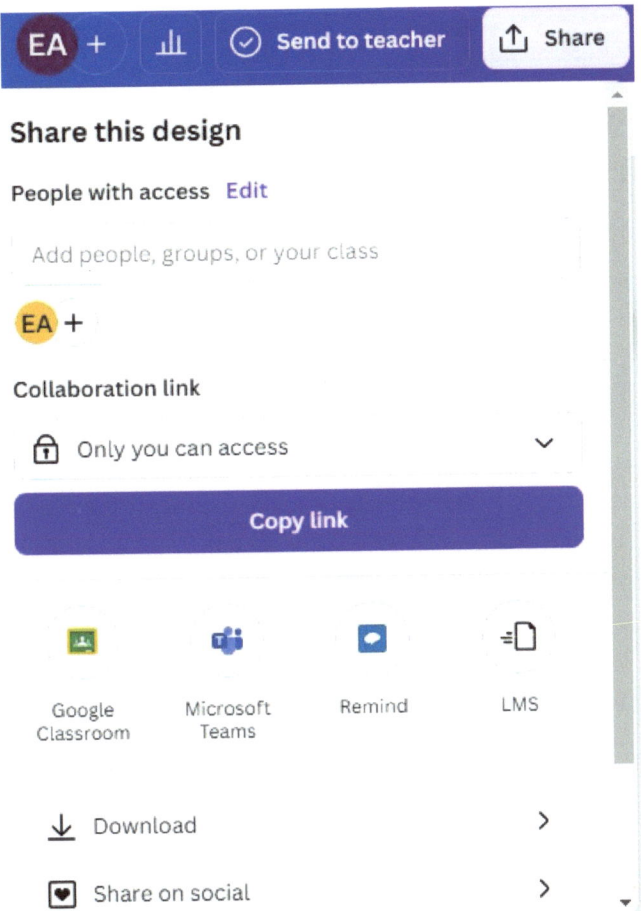

Example Project: Creating a School Poster

Let's walk through an example project to create a school poster:

1. **Choose a Template:** From the Canva dashboard, click on "Create a design" and select "Poster." Browse the templates and select one that fits your theme (e.g., a science fair poster).

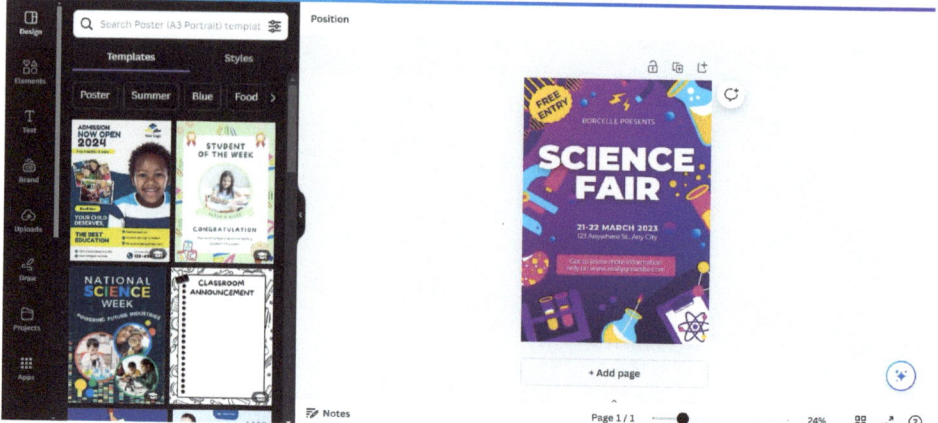

2. **Customize Text:** Click on the text boxes and edit the content to include the event name, date, time, location, and any other important details. Adjust the font, size, and color to make the text stand out.

3. **Add Images:** Replace the template images with relevant images from Canva's library or upload your own photos. For a science fair poster, you might include images of experiments, science equipment, or students participating.

4. **Adjust Colors:** Change the colors of elements to match your school's colors or the theme of the event. Use the color picker to choose complementary colors that enhance the overall design.

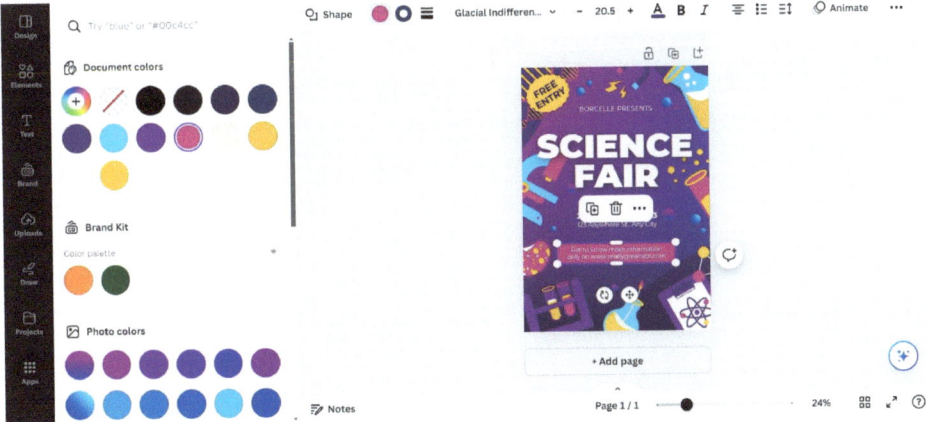

5. **Add Elements:** Add any additional elements, such as icons, shapes, or lines, to decorate the poster and make it more visually appealing. For example, you could add icons related to science, such as beakers or microscopes.

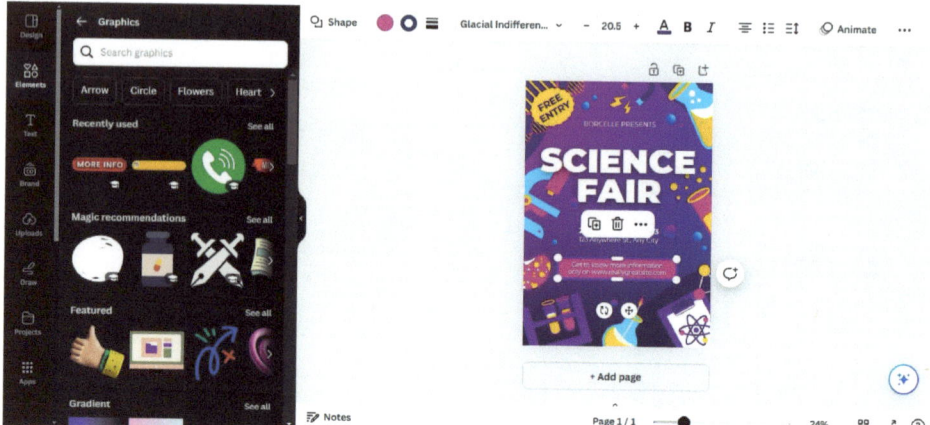

6. **Review and Finalize:** Ensure all elements are aligned and spaced correctly. Check that the text is readable and the images are clear. Make any final adjustments as needed.

7. **Save and Export:** Save your work, then download the poster as a PDF for printing or as a PNG for sharing online. You can also share the poster directly from Canva with your classmates or teachers.

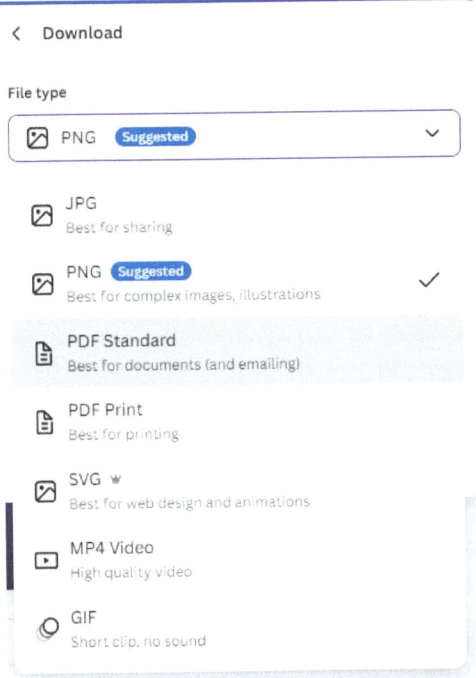

Creating your first design in Canva is a rewarding process that allows you to apply your creativity and design principles. By following these steps, you'll be able to produce a professional-quality design that effectively communicates your message and stands out from the crowd.

In the next chapter, we will explore advanced design techniques to help you take your Canva skills to the next level. Let's continue this creative journey and unlock even more possibilities with Canva!

Chapter 5: Advanced Design Techniques

Once you have mastered the basics of Canva, it's time to explore more advanced design techniques that can elevate your work to a professional level. This chapter will cover layering, masking, using grids, and other advanced features that can add depth and sophistication to your designs.

Layering

Layering is a powerful technique that allows you to stack multiple elements on top of each other to create complex and dynamic designs. Here's how to effectively use layering in Canva:

1. **Order of Layers:** The order in which elements are layered can affect the overall look of your design. To change the order of layers, right-click on an element and choose "Bring forward" or "Send backward." You can also use the position tool in the top right corner of the editor.

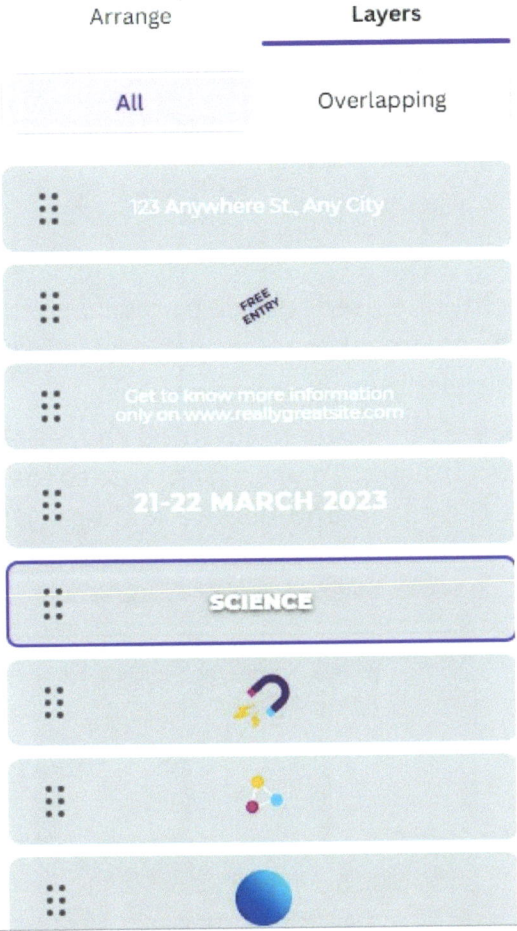

2. **Transparency:** Adjusting the transparency of elements can create interesting visual effects. Select an element, click on the transparency icon, and use the slider to adjust the opacity. This is useful for creating overlays and subtle backgrounds.

3. **Grouping:** Grouping elements together allows you to move and adjust multiple elements at once. Select the

elements you want to group, right-click, and choose "Group." This helps maintain the layout and alignment of complex designs.

Masking

Masking is a technique used to hide or reveal parts of an element, allowing you to create unique shapes and effects. Canva offers several tools for masking:

1. **Frames:** Frames are predefined shapes that you can use to mask images. To use a frame, go to the "Elements" tab, select "Frames," and choose a shape. Drag your image into the frame to mask it.

2. **Shapes:** You can use shapes to mask parts of your design. Place a shape over the area you want to hide, then adjust the color and transparency to blend it with the background.

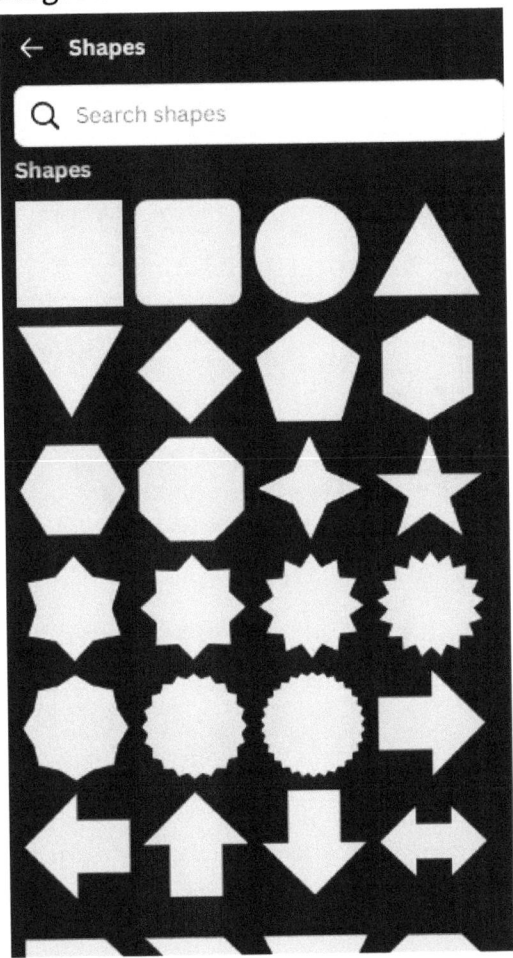

3. **Clipping Masks:** Canva doesn't have a direct clipping mask feature, but you can achieve similar effects by using frames and shapes creatively. For example, place a shape over an image, then duplicate the image and align it with the shape to create a masked effect.

Using Grids

Grids are an essential tool for creating structured and balanced designs. Canva provides a variety of grid layouts to help you align elements precisely:

1. **Adding Grids:** To add a grid, go to the "Elements" tab, select "Grids," and choose a layout. Grids can be used for photo collages, structured layouts, and aligning elements.

2. **Customizing Grids:** Once you've added a grid, you can customize it by adjusting the spacing, adding or removing cells, and resizing the grid. Click on the grid

and use the handles to make adjustments.

3. **Alignment:** Grids automatically align elements within each cell, ensuring a consistent and balanced design. Use grids to keep your layout organized and professional.

Advanced Typography

Typography is a critical aspect of design that can greatly influence the readability and visual appeal of your work. Here are some advanced typography techniques to enhance your designs:

1. **Font Pairing:** Combining different fonts can create a dynamic and visually interesting design. Choose fonts

that complement each other and create a hierarchy. Canva's text tool offers suggested font pairings to help you get started.

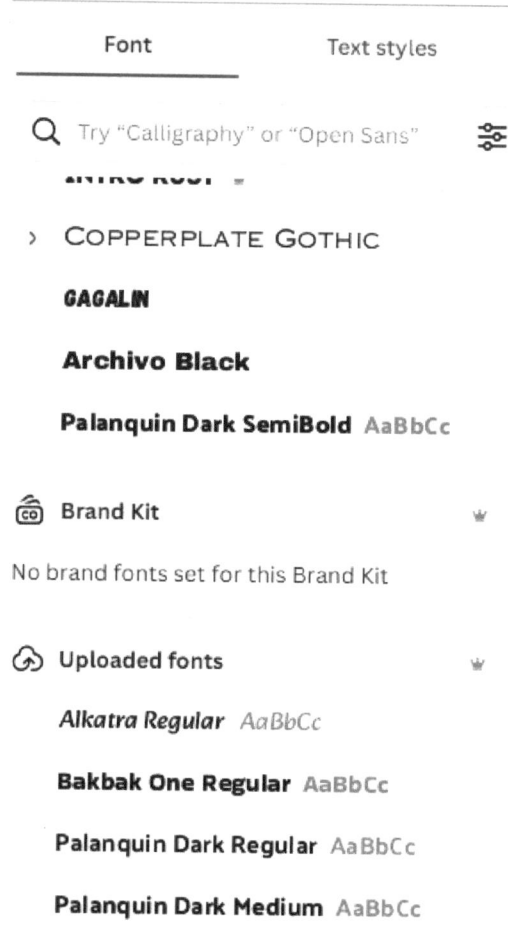

2. **Text Effects:** Use text effects like shadows, outlines, and highlights to make your text stand out. Click on the "Effects" button in the text toolbar to explore the options.

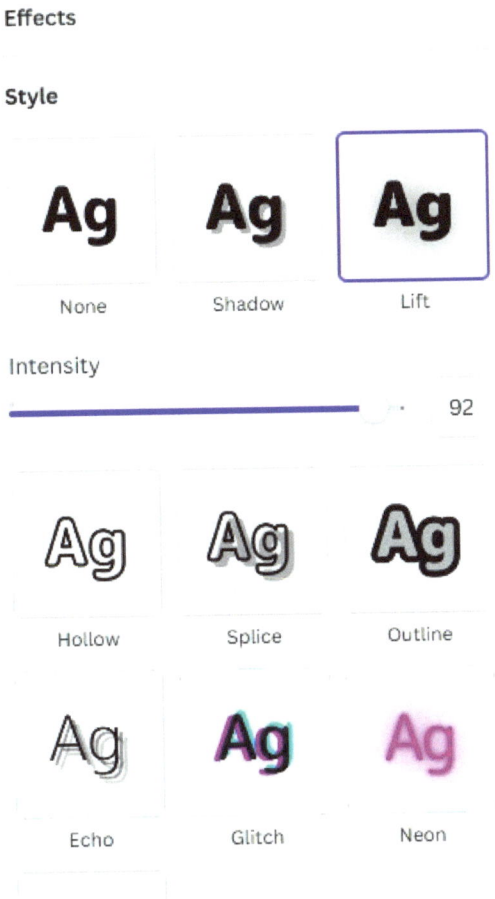

3. **Custom Lettering:** Create custom lettering by combining individual letters or words. Use Canva's elements and shapes to enhance your text and create unique typographic designs.

Advanced Image Editing

Canva offers a range of image editing tools that allow you to enhance and manipulate your images:

1. **Filters and Adjustments:** Apply filters to change the overall look of your image. Click on an image, then select "Filter" and choose from the available options. You

can also adjust settings like brightness, contrast, and saturation for a customized effect.

2. **Cropping and Resizing:** Use the crop tool to remove unwanted parts of an image. Click on an image, select "Crop," and adjust the handles to frame the desired area. You can also resize images by dragging the corners.

3. **Effects and Overlays:** Add effects like blur, vignette, and color overlays to create unique visuals. Click on an image, select "Effects," and explore the available options.

Creating Custom Templates

Once you've become comfortable with Canva's tools and features, you can create your own custom templates for future use:

1. **Design Your Template:** Start by creating a design that meets your specific needs. Customize the layout, fonts, colors, and elements to create a cohesive look.

2. **Save as Template:** Once your design is complete, click on the "File" menu and select "Save as template." This will save your design as a reusable template that you can access from the "Templates" tab.

3. **Use and Share:** Use your custom template for future projects to maintain consistency and save time. You can also share your templates with others by clicking on the "Share" button and sending a link.

By mastering these advanced design techniques, you'll be able to create sophisticated and professional-quality designs in Canva. In the next chapter, we'll explore the importance of branding and how to create a consistent brand identity using Canva's tools and features. Let's continue this creative journey and unlock even more possibilities with Canva!

Chapter 6: Branding and Consistency

Branding is a crucial aspect of design that involves creating a consistent and recognizable visual identity. In this chapter, we'll explore the importance of branding, the elements of a strong brand identity, and how to use Canva to create and maintain brand consistency.

Understanding Branding

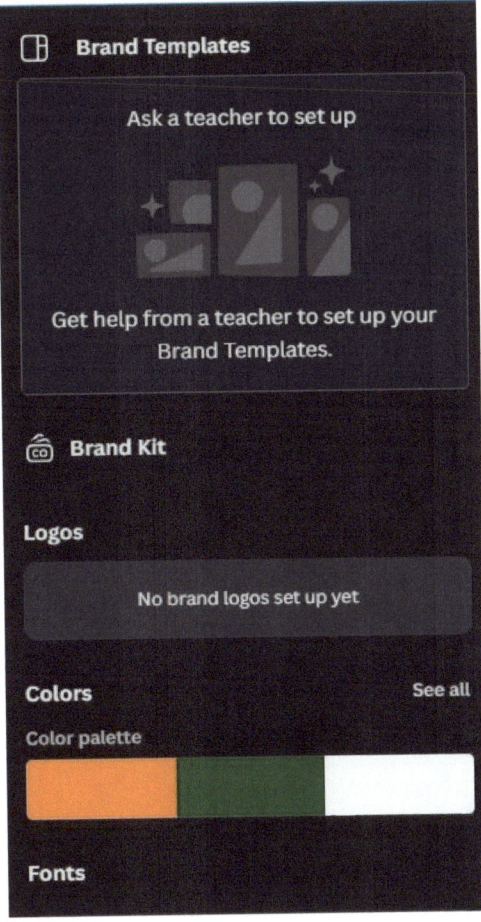

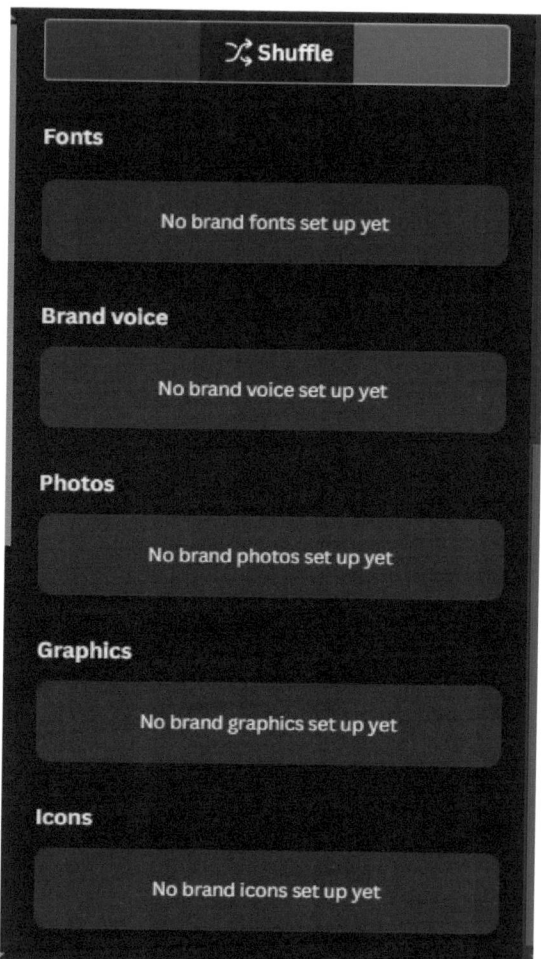

Branding is the process of creating a unique and cohesive visual identity that represents your organization, product, or personal brand. A strong brand identity helps build recognition, trust, and loyalty among your audience. Key elements of branding include:

1. **Logo:** A logo is a visual symbol that represents your brand. It should be simple, memorable, and versatile. Canva offers tools to design or customize logos that align with your brand identity.

2. **Color Palette:** Colors play a significant role in branding as they evoke emotions and convey messages. Choose a color palette that reflects your brand's personality and

values. Canva's color picker and palettes can help you create and apply your brand colors consistently.

3. **Typography:** Fonts are another important aspect of branding. Choose fonts that match your brand's tone and style. Canva offers a variety of fonts and allows you to upload custom fonts to maintain brand consistency.

4. **Imagery:** The images you use in your branding should reflect your brand's message and values. Choose images that are relevant and consistent with your brand's visual style. Canva's extensive library of photos and illustrations can help you find the right imagery.

5. **Voice and Tone:** Your brand's voice and tone refer to the way you communicate with your audience. This includes the language, style, and personality you convey through your messaging. Consistent voice and tone help build a strong brand identity.

Creating a Brand Kit in Canva

Canva's Brand Kit feature allows you to save and manage your brand assets in one place, making it easy to maintain consistency across all your designs. Here's how to create a Brand Kit:

1. **Access the Brand Kit:** From the Canva dashboard, click on the "Brand Kit" tab. This feature is available with Canva Pro accounts.

2. **Add Brand Colors:** Click on the "Add a new color" button to add your brand colors. You can enter the hex codes for precise color matching.

3. **Upload Logos:** Click on the "Upload a logo" button to upload your brand's logos. You can add multiple versions of your logo for different uses.

4. **Add Fonts:** Choose your brand's primary and secondary fonts from Canva's font library. If you have custom fonts, you can upload them to your Brand Kit.

Applying Your Brand Kit to Designs

Once you've created your Brand Kit, you can easily apply your brand assets to any design in Canva:

1. **Start a New Design:** Create a new design from the Canva dashboard.

2. **Access Brand Assets:** Click on the "Brand Kit" tab in the editor to access your brand colors, logos, and fonts.

3. **Apply Brand Colors:** Use the color picker to select your brand colors and apply them to elements in your design.

4. **Add Logos:** Drag and drop your logo from the Brand Kit into your design. Resize and position it as needed.

5. **Use Brand Fonts:** Select your brand fonts from the font dropdown menu and apply them to your text elements.

Maintaining Brand Consistency

Consistency is key to building a strong brand identity. Here are some tips for maintaining brand consistency in your designs:

1. **Stick to Your Brand Guidelines:** Follow your brand guidelines for colors, fonts, logos, and imagery. Canva's Brand Kit makes it easy to apply these guidelines consistently.

2. **Use Templates:** Create and use templates for recurring design projects. This ensures that your designs maintain a consistent look and feel.

3. **Review and Approve:** Before finalizing any design, review it to ensure it adheres to your brand guidelines. If you're working with a team, establish a review and approval process.

4. **Train Your Team:** Educate your team members on your brand guidelines and the importance of consistency. Provide them with access to your Brand Kit and templates.

Example Project: Creating a Social Media Post

Let's create a branded social media post using Canva's Brand Kit:

1. **Choose a Template:** From the Canva dashboard, click on

"Create a design" and select "Instagram Post." Browse the templates and select one that fits your theme.

2. **Apply Brand Colors:** Click on the "Brand Kit" tab, select your brand colors, and apply them to the elements in the template.

3. **Add Logo:** Drag your logo from the Brand Kit into the design. Resize and position it appropriately.

4. **Use Brand Fonts:** Select your brand fonts from the font dropdown menu and apply them to the text elements in the template.

5. **Customize Content:** Edit the text to include your message, adjust the imagery to fit your brand, and make any final adjustments.

6. **Review and Export:** Review the design to ensure it adheres to your brand guidelines, then download or share it directly from Canva.

By creating a strong and consistent brand identity, you can effectively communicate your message and build a loyal audience. In the next chapter, we will explore the importance of visual storytelling and how to create compelling visual narratives using Canva. Let's continue this creative journey and unlock even more possibilities with Canva!

Chapter 7: Visual Storytelling

Visual storytelling is a powerful way to convey messages, evoke emotions, and engage your audience. In this chapter, we'll explore the principles of visual storytelling, the elements that make a compelling story, and how to use Canva to create impactful visual narratives.

Understanding Visual Storytelling

Visual storytelling combines visual elements with narrative techniques to tell a story. It's an effective way to communicate complex ideas, capture attention, and make a lasting impression. Key components of visual storytelling include:

1. **Characters:** Characters are the central figures in your story. They can be people, animals, or objects that play a role in your narrative. Well-developed characters help create a connection with your audience.

2. **Setting:** The setting provides the context for your story. It includes the time, place, and environment where the story unfolds. A well-defined setting helps immerse your audience in the narrative.

3. **Plot:** The plot is the sequence of events that make up your story. It includes the beginning, middle, and end, as well as the conflict and resolution. A strong plot keeps your audience engaged and interested.

4. **Theme:** The theme is the underlying message or main idea of your story. It's the point you want to convey to your audience. A clear and compelling theme adds depth to your narrative.

5. **Visual Elements:** Visual elements include images,

illustrations, colors, typography, and layout. These elements work together to support and enhance your narrative.

Creating Visual Stories in Canva

Canva provides the tools and resources to create compelling visual stories. Here's how to use Canva to bring your stories to life:

1. **Define Your Story:** Start by outlining the key components of your story: characters, setting, plot, and theme. Decide on the main message you want to convey and the emotions you want to evoke.

2. **Choose a Format:** Select the format for your visual story. This could be a social media post, infographic, presentation, or video. Canva offers templates for various formats to help you get started.

3. **Gather Visual Assets:** Collect the images, illustrations, icons, and other visual elements you need for your story. Canva's library provides a wide range of assets, or you can upload your own.

4. **Create a Storyboard:** A storyboard is a visual outline of your story. Use Canva's grid and frame tools to create a storyboard that maps out the sequence of events and visual elements.

5. **Design Each Scene:** Design each scene of your story, focusing on the key components. Use Canva's design tools to add characters, settings, and plot elements. Pay attention to the visual hierarchy and flow to guide your audience through the narrative.

6. **Add Text and Captions:** Use text and captions to enhance your visual story. Choose fonts and colors that complement your visuals and support your narrative. Keep text concise and impactful.

7. **Use Visual Effects:** Apply visual effects, such as filters, overlays, and animations, to add depth and interest to your story. Canva offers a variety of effects to enhance

your visuals.

8. **Review and Refine:** Review your visual story to ensure it's clear, engaging, and aligned with your message. Make any necessary adjustments to improve the overall impact.

Example Project: Creating an Infographic

Let's create an infographic to tell a visual story about the importance of recycling:

1. **Define Your Story:** The theme is the importance of recycling. Characters could include a family, recycling bins, and nature. The setting is a community. The plot includes the problem (waste pollution), the action (recycling), and the resolution (clean environment).

2. **Choose a Template:** From the Canva dashboard, click on "Create a design" and select "Infographic." Browse the templates and select one that fits your theme.

3. **Gather Visual Assets:** Search for images of a family, recycling bins, and nature in Canva's library. Upload any additional assets you need.

4. **Create a Storyboard:** Use a grid layout to map out the sequence of events: introduction, problem, action, and resolution.

5. **Design Each Scene:** Design each section of the infographic, adding characters, settings, and plot elements. Use visual hierarchy to guide the audience's attention.

6. **Add Text and Captions:** Add concise text and captions to explain each part of the story. Use a consistent font and color scheme.

7. **Use Visual Effects:** Apply filters and overlays to enhance the visuals. Add icons and illustrations to support the narrative.

8. **Review and Refine:** Review the infographic to ensure it's

clear, engaging, and effectively conveys the importance of recycling. Make any necessary adjustments.

By mastering the art of visual storytelling, you can create engaging and impactful designs that resonate with your audience. In the next chapter, we will explore the use of Canva for presentations and how to create professional and compelling slideshows. Let's continue this creative journey and unlock even more possibilities with Canva!

Chapter 8: Designing Presentations

Presentations are a powerful tool for communicating ideas, sharing information, and persuading audiences. In this chapter, we'll explore how to create professional and compelling presentations using Canva, including tips for designing effective slides, incorporating visual elements, and delivering your presentation with confidence.

Principles of Effective Presentations

Creating an effective presentation involves more than just putting together a series of slides. Here are some key principles to keep in mind:

1. **Clarity:** Ensure your message is clear and easy to understand. Avoid clutter and focus on one main idea per slide.

2. **Visual Appeal:** Use visuals to enhance your message and engage your audience. Incorporate images, icons, charts, and graphs to illustrate your points.

3. **Consistency:** Maintain a consistent look and feel throughout your presentation. Use the same fonts, colors, and styles on all slides.

4. **Engagement:** Engage your audience by using interactive elements, asking questions, and encouraging participation. Make your presentation dynamic and interesting.

5. **Simplicity:** Keep your slides simple and focused. Avoid overloading them with too much information or too many elements.

Creating a Presentation in Canva

Canva provides a range of tools and templates to help you create professional presentations. Here's how to get started:

1. **Choose a Template:** From the Canva dashboard, click on "Create a design" and select "Presentation." Browse the templates and choose one that fits your theme and style.

2. **Customize the Slides:** Customize each slide to fit your content. Add text, images, charts, and other elements to convey your message. Use Canva's drag-and-drop interface to easily arrange and adjust elements.

3. **Add Visual Elements:** Incorporate visual elements such as images, icons, and illustrations to enhance your slides. Canva's library offers a wide range of visuals to choose from.

4. **Use Consistent Fonts and Colors:** Apply your brand fonts and colors to maintain consistency. Use Canva's Brand Kit if you have one, or manually select your preferred fonts and colors.

5. **Add Transitions and Animations:** Use transitions and animations to add movement and interest to your slides. Click on the "Animate" button to choose from a variety of options.

6. **Review and Refine:** Review your presentation to ensure it's clear, engaging, and professional. Make any necessary adjustments to improve the overall quality.

Tips for Delivering Your Presentation

Creating a great presentation is only part of the process. Delivering it effectively is equally important. Here are some tips for delivering a successful presentation:

1. **Practice:** Practice your presentation multiple times to become familiar with the content and flow. This will help you deliver it confidently and smoothly.

2. **Engage Your Audience:** Make eye contact, ask questions, and encourage participation. Engage your audience to

keep their attention and make your presentation more interactive.

3. **Use Visual Cues:** Use visual cues on your slides to guide your audience's attention. Highlight key points, use bullet points, and incorporate visuals to support your message.

4. **Keep it Simple:** Avoid reading directly from your slides. Use them as a guide and expand on the points verbally. Keep your slides simple and focused.

5. **Manage Your Time:** Keep an eye on the time and ensure you stay within the allotted timeframe. Practice timing your presentation to avoid running over.

Example Project: Creating a Business Presentation

Let's create a business presentation to pitch a new product:

1. **Choose a Template:** From the Canva dashboard, click on "Create a design" and select "Presentation." Browse the business templates and select one that fits your theme.

2. **Customize the Slides:** Customize the title slide with your company name and logo. Add slides for the product overview, features, benefits, market analysis, and conclusion.

3. **Add Visual Elements:** Incorporate images of the product, charts to show market trends, and icons to highlight key features. Use Canva's library to find suitable visuals.

4. **Use Consistent Fonts and Colors:** Apply your brand fonts and colors to maintain consistency. Ensure all slides have a cohesive look and feel.

5. **Add Transitions and Animations:** Use subtle transitions and animations to add movement to your slides. Avoid overusing animations to keep the presentation professional.

6. **Review and Refine:** Review your presentation to ensure

it's clear, engaging, and effectively communicates your message. Make any necessary adjustments.

By following these principles and using Canva's tools, you can create professional and compelling presentations that effectively communicate your message and engage your audience. In the next chapter, we will explore the use of Canva for creating social media graphics and how to design eye-catching posts that stand out. Let's continue this creative journey and unlock even more possibilities with Canva!

Chapter 9: Designing Social Media Graphics

Social media is a powerful platform for reaching and engaging with your audience. In this chapter, we'll explore how to use Canva to create eye-catching social media graphics that stand out in the crowded online space. We'll cover best practices for designing social media posts, tips for different platforms, and how to maintain a consistent brand presence across all your social media channels.

Best Practices for Social Media Graphics

Creating effective social media graphics involves understanding the specific requirements and best practices for each platform. Here are some general tips to keep in mind:

1. **Know Your Audience:** Understand your audience's preferences and interests. Design graphics that resonate with them and align with your brand's voice and message.

2. **Use High-Quality Images:** High-quality images are essential for creating professional-looking graphics. Use Canva's library of stock photos or upload your own.

3. **Keep It Simple:** Social media users often scroll quickly through their feeds. Keep your designs simple, clear, and focused on one main message.

4. **Use Eye-Catching Colors:** Bright, contrasting colors can help your posts stand out. Use your brand's color palette to maintain consistency.

5. **Incorporate Your Logo:** Always include your logo to reinforce brand recognition. Place it in a consistent location on all your graphics.

6. **Optimize for Each Platform:** Different social media

platforms have different image size requirements. Make sure to resize your graphics for each platform to ensure they display correctly.

Creating Social Media Graphics in Canva

Canva makes it easy to create professional social media graphics with its range of templates and design tools. Here's how to get started:

1. **Choose a Template:** From the Canva dashboard, click on "Create a design" and select the social media platform you're designing for (e.g., Instagram Post, Facebook Post, Twitter Post). Browse the templates and choose one that fits your theme and style.

2. **Customize the Design:** Customize the template with your content. Add text, images, icons, and other elements to convey your message. Use Canva's drag-and-drop interface to easily arrange and adjust elements.

3. **Apply Your Brand Elements:** Use your brand fonts, colors, and logo to maintain consistency. Canva's Brand Kit can help streamline this process.

4. **Add Visual Effects:** Enhance your graphics with visual effects like filters, overlays, and animations. Click on the "Effects" button to explore the available options.

5. **Resize for Different Platforms:** Use Canva's "Resize" feature to quickly adjust your design for different social media platforms. This ensures your graphics look great on all channels.

6. **Review and Export:** Review your design to ensure it's clear, engaging, and aligned with your brand. Download your graphic or share it directly to your social media accounts from Canva.

Tips for Different Social Media Platforms

Each social media platform has its own unique characteristics and best practices. Here are some tips for designing graphics for the most popular platforms:

Instagram

1. **Square and Vertical Images:** Instagram primarily uses square (1080x1080 pixels) and vertical (1080x1350 pixels) images.

Ensure your designs fit these dimensions.

2. **Visual Storytelling:** Use carousel posts to tell a story or share a series of images. This format encourages users to swipe through multiple images.

3. **Hashtags and Captions:** Incorporate relevant hashtags and engaging captions to increase visibility and engagement. Use Canva's text tools to create eye-catching captions.

Facebook

1. **High-Quality Images:** Use high-quality images that are at least 1200x630 pixels for optimal display. Facebook often compresses images, so starting with high-quality visuals is important.

2. **Event Promotions:** Create eye-catching event banners and cover photos. Use Canva's templates for events to design engaging graphics.

3. **Ad Graphics:** If you're creating graphics for Facebook ads, ensure they comply with Facebook's ad guidelines. Keep text to a minimum to avoid ad rejection.

Twitter

1. **Horizontal Images:** Twitter uses horizontal images (1600x900 pixels). Ensure your designs fit this dimension to display correctly.

2. **Concise Messaging:** Twitter's character limit encourages concise messaging. Use clear and impactful text in your graphics.

3. **Engagement:** Create graphics that encourage retweets, likes, and comments. Use Canva's icons and illustrations to add interactive elements.

LinkedIn

1. **Professional Tone:** LinkedIn is a professional network, so maintain a polished and professional tone in your graphics. Use clean designs and sophisticated color palettes.

2. **Article Thumbnails:** Create engaging thumbnails for LinkedIn articles. Use Canva's templates to design professional-looking covers.

3. **Company Updates:** Share company updates and industry news with well-designed graphics. Incorporate your brand elements to maintain consistency.

Example Project: Creating an Instagram Post

Let's create an engaging Instagram post to promote a new product launch:

1. **Choose a Template:** From the Canva dashboard, click on "Create a design" and select "Instagram Post." Browse the templates and choose one that fits your theme.
2. **Customize the Design:** Customize the template with your product image, launch date, and key features. Use Canva's text tools to create an eye-catching caption.
3. **Apply Brand Elements:** Use your brand fonts, colors, and logo to maintain consistency. Adjust the colors and fonts to match your brand's style.
4. **Add Visual Effects:** Enhance your graphic with filters and overlays. Click on the "Effects" button to explore the available options.
5. **Resize for Other Platforms:** Use Canva's "Resize" feature to adjust your design for Facebook, Twitter, and LinkedIn. This ensures your launch announcement is consistent across all channels.
6. **Review and Export:** Review your design to ensure it's clear, engaging, and aligned with your brand. Download your graphic or share it directly to your Instagram account from Canva.

By mastering the art of social media graphics, you can effectively engage your audience and promote your brand across various platforms. In the next chapter, we will explore the use of Canva for creating marketing materials and how to design brochures, flyers, and posters that captivate your audience. Let's continue this creative journey and unlock even more possibilities with Canva!

Chapter 10: Designing Marketing Materials

Marketing materials are essential tools for promoting your business, products, or services. In this chapter, we'll explore how to use Canva to design brochures, flyers, posters, and other marketing materials that captivate your audience and drive engagement. We'll cover best practices for designing effective marketing materials, tips for different types of materials, and how to maintain a consistent brand presence.

Best Practices for Marketing Materials

Creating effective marketing materials involves understanding the specific requirements and best practices for each type of material. Here are some general tips to keep in mind:

1. **Know Your Purpose:** Clearly define the purpose of your marketing material. Are you promoting a product, announcing an event, or providing information? Tailor your design to meet this purpose.

2. **Target Your Audience:** Understand your audience's preferences and interests. Design materials that resonate with them and align with your brand's voice and message.

3. **Use High-Quality Images:** High-quality images are essential for creating professional-looking marketing materials. Use Canva's library of stock photos or upload your own.

4. **Clear Call to Action (CTA):** Include a clear and compelling call to action. What do you want your audience to do after seeing your material? Make this action easy to understand and follow.

5. **Consistent Branding:** Maintain a consistent look and feel across all your marketing materials. Use your brand fonts,

colors, and logo to reinforce brand recognition.

6. **Simplicity:** Keep your designs simple and focused. Avoid clutter and make sure your main message is clear and easy to understand.

Creating Marketing Materials in Canva

Canva makes it easy to create professional marketing materials with its range of templates and design tools. Here's how to get started:

1. **Choose a Template:** From the Canva dashboard, click on "Create a design" and select the type of marketing material you're designing (e.g., Brochure, Flyer, Poster). Browse the templates and choose one that fits your theme and style.

2. **Customize the Design:** Customize the template with your content. Add text, images, icons, and other elements to convey your message. Use Canva's drag-and-drop interface to easily arrange and adjust elements.

3. **Apply Your Brand Elements:** Use your brand fonts, colors, and logo to maintain consistency. Canva's Brand Kit can help streamline this process.

4. **Add Visual Effects:** Enhance your materials with visual effects like filters, overlays, and animations. Click on the "Effects" button to explore the available options.

5. **Review and Export:** Review your design to ensure it's clear, engaging, and aligned with your brand. Download your material or print it directly from Canva.

Tips for Different Types of Marketing Materials

Each type of marketing material has its own unique characteristics and best practices. Here are some tips for designing the most common types of marketing materials:

Brochures

1. **Organize Content:** Brochures often contain a lot of information. Organize your content into sections with clear headings and subheadings.

2. **Use High-Quality Images:** Include high-quality images that illustrate your message. Use Canva's layout tools to arrange images and text in a balanced way.

3. **Include Contact Information:** Make sure to include your

contact information, such as phone number, email, and website. Place this information in a prominent location.

Flyers

1. **Catchy Headline:** Use a catchy headline to grab attention. Make it bold and easy to read.

2. **Highlight Key Information:** Focus on the key information you want to convey. Use bullet points, icons, and images to make the flyer easy to scan.

3. **Clear CTA:** Include a clear and compelling call to action. Make sure it stands out on the flyer.

Posters

1. **Bold Design:** Posters need to grab attention from a distance. Use bold colors, large text, and striking images.

2. **Simple and Focused:** Keep your design simple and focused on one main message. Avoid clutter and make sure your text is easy to read.

3. **Consistent Branding:** Use your brand fonts, colors, and logo to maintain consistency.

Example Project: Creating a Promotional Flyer

Let's create an engaging promotional flyer for a new product launch:

1. **Choose a Template:** From the Canva dashboard, click on "Create a design" and select "Flyer." Browse the templates and choose one that fits your theme.

2. **Customize the Design:** Customize the template with your product image, launch date, and key features. Use Canva's text tools to create an eye-catching headline.

3. **Apply Brand Elements:** Use your brand fonts, colors, and logo to maintain consistency. Adjust the colors and fonts to match your brand's style.

4. **Add Visual Effects:** Enhance your flyer with filters and overlays. Click on the "Effects" button to explore the available options.

5. **Review and Export:** Review your design to ensure it's clear, engaging, and aligned with your brand. Download your flyer or print it directly from Canva.

By mastering the art of marketing materials, you can effectively promote your business and engage your audience. In the next chapter, we will explore the use of Canva for creating print materials and how to design business cards, letterheads, and other printed items. Let's continue this creative journey and unlock even more possibilities with Canva!

Chapter 11: Designing Print Materials

Print materials remain a vital part of marketing and communication strategies. In this chapter, we'll explore how to use Canva to design business cards, letterheads, and other printed items that make a strong impression. We'll cover best practices for designing effective print materials, tips for different types of print items, and how to maintain a consistent brand presence.

Best Practices for Print Materials

Creating effective print materials involves understanding the specific requirements and best practices for each type of item. Here are some general tips to keep in mind:

1. **High-Resolution Images:** Print materials require high-resolution images to ensure they look sharp and professional. Canva allows you to download designs in print-quality resolution.

2. **Consistent Branding:** Maintain a consistent look and feel across all your print materials. Use your brand fonts, colors, and logo to reinforce brand recognition.

3. **Clear Layouts:** Keep your layouts clean and easy to read. Avoid clutter and ensure that your key information is easy to find.

4. **Professional Typography:** Use professional fonts and typographic hierarchy to create a polished look. Ensure that your text is legible and well-organized.

5. **Appropriate Paper and Printing:** Consider the type of paper and printing method that will best suit your design. Canva offers various printing options to meet your needs.

Creating Print Materials in Canva

Canva makes it easy to create professional print materials with its range of templates and design tools. Here's how to get started:

1. **Choose a Template:** From the Canva dashboard, click on "Create a design" and select the type of print material you're designing (e.g., Business Card, Letterhead, Poster). Browse the templates and choose one that fits your theme and style.

2. **Customize the Design:** Customize the template with your content. Add text, images, icons, and other elements to convey your message. Use Canva's drag-and-drop interface to easily arrange and adjust elements.

3. **Apply Your Brand Elements:** Use your brand fonts, colors, and logo to maintain consistency. Canva's Brand Kit can help streamline this process.

4. **Add Visual Effects:** Enhance your materials with visual effects like filters, overlays, and illustrations. Click on the "Effects" button to explore the available options.

5. **Review and Export:** Review your design to ensure it's clear, engaging, and aligned with your brand. Download your material in print-quality resolution or use Canva's printing services.

Tips for Different Types of Print Materials

Each type of print material has its own unique characteristics and best practices. Here are some tips for designing the most common types of print materials:

Business Cards

1. **Keep It Simple:** Business cards should be simple and easy to read. Include your name, title, contact information, and logo.

2. **Professional Design:** Use professional fonts and colors. Ensure that your design reflects your brand's identity and professionalism.

3. **High-Quality Printing:** Choose a high-quality paper and printing method. Canva offers various options to ensure your business cards look professional.

Letterheads

1. **Consistent Branding:** Use your brand fonts, colors, and logo to maintain consistency across all your letterheads.

2. **Professional Layout:** Keep the layout clean and professional. Include your company name, address, phone number, and email.

3. **High-Quality Paper:** Choose a high-quality paper for printing

your letterheads. Canva's printing services offer various options to meet your needs.

Posters

1. **Bold Design:** Posters need to grab attention from a distance. Use bold colors, large text, and striking images.

2. **Clear Message:** Keep your message clear and focused. Ensure that your main message is easy to read and understand.

3. **High-Quality Printing:** Choose a high-quality paper and printing method. Canva offers various options to ensure your posters look professional.

Example Project: Creating a Business Card

Let's create a professional business card for a new entrepreneur:

1. **Choose a Template:** From the Canva dashboard, click on "Create a design" and select "Business Card." Browse the templates and choose one that fits your theme.

2. **Customize the Design:** Customize the template with your name, title, contact information, and logo. Use Canva's text tools to create a professional layout.

3. **Apply Brand Elements:** Use your brand fonts, colors, and logo to maintain consistency. Adjust the colors and fonts to match your brand's style.

4. **Add Visual Effects:** Enhance your business card with subtle visual effects like filters and overlays. Click on the "Effects" button to explore the available options.

5. **Review and Export:** Review your design to ensure it's clear, professional, and aligned with your brand. Download your business card in print-quality resolution or use Canva's printing services.

By mastering the art of print materials, you can effectively promote your business and make a strong impression on your audience. In the next chapter, we will explore the use of Canva for creating merchandise and how to design products like t-shirts, mugs, and more. Let's continue this creative journey and unlock even more possibilities with Canva!

Chapter 12: Designing Merchandise

Creating custom merchandise is a great way to promote your brand and engage your audience. In this chapter, we'll explore how to use Canva to design products like t-shirts, mugs, tote bags, and more. We'll cover best practices for designing effective merchandise, tips for different types of products, and how to maintain a consistent brand presence.

Best Practices for Merchandise Design

Creating effective merchandise involves understanding the specific requirements and best practices for each type of product. Here are some general tips to keep in mind:

1. **Know Your Audience:** Understand your audience's preferences and interests. Design products that resonate with them and align with your brand's voice and message.
2. **Use High-Quality Images:** High-quality images are essential for creating professional-looking merchandise. Use Canva's library of stock photos or upload your own.
3. **Simple and Bold Designs:** Merchandise often benefits from simple and bold designs that are easy to recognize and remember.
4. **Consistent Branding:** Maintain a consistent look and feel across all your merchandise. Use your brand fonts, colors, and logo to reinforce brand recognition.
5. **Consider the Product:** Tailor your design to fit the specific product. Consider how the design will look on different surfaces and materials.

Creating Merchandise in Canva

Canva makes it easy to create professional merchandise with its range of templates and design tools. Here's how to get started:

1. **Choose a Template:** From the Canva dashboard, click on

"Create a design" and select the type of merchandise you're designing (e.g., T-shirt, Mug, Tote Bag). Browse the templates and choose one that fits your theme and style.

2. **Customize the Design:** Customize the template with your content. Add text, images, icons, and other elements to convey your message. Use Canva's drag-and-drop interface to easily arrange and adjust elements.

3. **Apply Your Brand Elements:** Use your brand fonts, colors, and logo to maintain consistency. Canva's Brand Kit can help streamline this process.

4. **Add Visual Effects:** Enhance your merchandise with visual effects like filters, overlays, and illustrations. Click on the "Effects" button to explore the available options.

5. **Review and Export:** Review your design to ensure it's clear, engaging, and aligned with your brand. Download your design in the appropriate format for printing or use Canva's printing services.

Tips for Different Types of Merchandise

Each type of merchandise has its own unique characteristics and best practices. Here are some tips for designing the most common types of merchandise:

T-Shirts

1. **Simple and Bold Designs:** Use simple and bold designs that are easy to recognize and remember. Avoid overly complex designs that may not print well.

2. **High-Quality Images:** Ensure your images are high-resolution to avoid pixelation. Canva allows you to download designs in high-quality resolution.

3. **Consistent Branding:** Use your brand fonts, colors, and logo to maintain consistency.

Mugs

1. **Focus on the Center:** Place your main design in the center of the mug. This ensures it will be visible when the mug is held.

2. **Simple and Clear Designs:** Use simple and clear designs that are easy to read and understand. Avoid overly complex designs that may not print well.

3. **High-Quality Images:** Ensure your images are high-resolution to avoid pixelation.

Tote Bags

1. **Bold and Eye-Catching Designs:** Use bold and eye-catching designs that will stand out when the tote bag is carried.
2. **High-Quality Images:** Ensure your images are high-resolution to avoid pixelation.
3. **Consistent Branding:** Use your brand fonts, colors, and logo to maintain consistency.

Example Project: Creating a T-Shirt Design

Let's create an engaging t-shirt design for a new product launch:

1. **Choose a Template:** From the Canva dashboard, click on "Create a design" and select "T-shirt." Browse the templates and choose one that fits your theme.
2. **Customize the Design:** Customize the template with your product image, launch date, and key features. Use Canva's text tools to create an eye-catching design.
3. **Apply Brand Elements:** Use your brand fonts, colors, and logo to maintain consistency. Adjust the colors and fonts to match your brand's style.
4. **Add Visual Effects:** Enhance your t-shirt design with filters and overlays. Click on the "Effects" button to explore the available options.
5. **Review and Export:** Review your design to ensure it's clear, engaging, and aligned with your brand. Download your design in the

By mastering the art of designing merchandise, you can effectively promote your brand and engage your audience through tangible products. In the next chapter, we will explore advanced design techniques in Canva, including animations, presentations, and more. Let's continue this creative journey and unlock even more possibilities with Canva!

Chapter 13: Advanced Design Techniques

Canva offers a wide range of advanced design techniques that can take your creations to the next level. In this chapter, we'll explore how to use Canva for animations, presentations, infographics, and more. We'll cover best practices for each type of design, tips for creating visually appealing content, and how to leverage Canva's tools for maximum impact.

Animations

Animations can bring your designs to life and capture your audience's attention. Here's how to create animations in Canva:

1. **Choose an Animation Template:** From the Canva dashboard, click on "Create a design" and select "Animation." Browse the templates and choose one that fits your project.

2. **Customize the Animation:** Customize the template with your content. Add text, images, and icons to create your animated design. Canva's animation tools allow you to animate text, elements, and backgrounds.

3. **Preview and Adjust:** Preview your animation to ensure it flows smoothly and effectively communicates your message. Make any necessary adjustments to timing and effects.

4. **Download or Share:** Download your animated design as a video file or share it directly to social media platforms from Canva.

Presentations

Creating visually appealing presentations is essential for effectively communicating your ideas. Here's how to create presentations in Canva:

1. **Choose a Presentation Template:** From the Canva dashboard, click on "Create a design" and select "Presentation." Browse the templates and choose one that fits your topic and audience.

2. **Customize the Presentation:** Customize the template with your content. Add text, images, charts, and other elements to convey your message. Use Canva's drag-and-drop interface to arrange and format your slides.

3. **Apply Design Principles:** Use design principles such as contrast, repetition, alignment, and proximity to create visually appealing slides. Ensure that your slides are easy to read and understand.

4. **Add Transitions and Animations:** Enhance your presentation with slide transitions and animations to keep your audience engaged. Use Canva's animation tools to animate elements within your slides.

5. **Review and Present:** Review your presentation to ensure it's clear, cohesive, and visually appealing. Practice your presentation delivery to ensure you effectively communicate your message.

Infographics

Infographics are powerful tools for presenting complex information in a visually engaging way. Here's how to create infographics in Canva:

1. **Choose an Infographic Template:** From the Canva dashboard, click on "Create a design" and select "Infographic." Browse the templates and choose one that fits your data and narrative.

2. **Customize the Infographic:** Customize the template with your data. Use Canva's charts, graphs, icons, and illustrations to visualize your information. Arrange elements to create a clear flow of information.

3. **Apply Visual Hierarchy:** Use visual hierarchy to

prioritize information and guide the viewer's attention. Use color, size, and contrast to distinguish between different data points.

4. **Add Annotations and Descriptions:** Include annotations and descriptions to provide context and insights into your data. Use Canva's text tools to add labels and explanations.

5. **Review and Export:** Review your infographic to ensure it effectively communicates your message. Download your infographic as an image file or share it directly from Canva.

Example Project: Creating an Animated Social Media Post

Let's create an animated social media post to promote a special offer:

1. **Choose an Animation Template:** From the Canva dashboard, click on "Create a design" and select "Animation." Browse the templates and choose one that fits your promotion.

2. **Customize the Animation:** Customize the template with your offer details, images, and call to action. Use Canva's animation tools to animate text and elements.

3. **Preview and Adjust:** Preview your animation to ensure it flows smoothly and effectively captures attention. Adjust timing and effects as needed.

4. **Download or Share:** Download your animated social media post as a video file or share it directly to your social media accounts from Canva.

By mastering advanced design techniques in Canva, you can create compelling visuals that engage your audience and enhance your brand's presence. In the next chapter, we will explore collaboration and workflow tips in Canva, including team collaboration, sharing designs, and managing projects. Let's continue this creative journey and unlock even more possibilities with Canva!

Chapter 14: Collaboration and Workflow in Canva

Effective collaboration and streamlined workflows are crucial for teams working on design projects. In this chapter, we'll explore how Canva facilitates collaboration, sharing designs, and managing projects efficiently. We'll cover best practices for team collaboration, tips for sharing designs securely, and how to use Canva's features to enhance workflow productivity.

Team Collaboration in Canva

Canva offers robust features for team collaboration, allowing multiple users to work together on designs in real-time. Here's how to collaborate effectively in Canva:

1. **Create a Team:** Start by creating a team in Canva. Invite team members to join and assign roles based on their permissions (e.g., Editor, Viewer).

2. **Real-Time Editing:** Collaborators can edit designs simultaneously, seeing changes in real-time. This allows for seamless collaboration and faster iteration.

3. **Commenting and Feedback:** Use Canva's commenting feature to leave feedback directly on designs. Collaborators can respond to comments, facilitating communication.

4. **Version History:** Canva automatically saves versions of your designs, allowing you to revert to previous versions if needed. This feature helps maintain project integrity.

5. **Shared Folders:** Organize designs into shared folders for

easy access and collaboration. Team members can view and edit designs within these folders as needed.

Sharing Designs Securely

Sharing designs securely is essential to protect intellectual property and ensure confidentiality. Here's how to share designs securely in Canva:

1. **Share Link Permissions:** Control access to your designs by setting permissions when sharing links. Choose whether recipients can view, comment, or edit the design.

2. **Password Protection:** Optionally, add password protection to shared links for an extra layer of security.

3. **Expiration Dates:** Set expiration dates for shared links to limit access to your designs after a specified period.

4. **Download Permissions:** Specify whether recipients can download designs when sharing links. This helps you control distribution and usage.

5. **Embedding Options:** Embed Canva designs directly into websites or presentations securely. Customize embedding settings to fit your needs.

Workflow Productivity with Canva

Canva offers features and integrations to enhance workflow productivity for design projects. Here are some tips to maximize workflow productivity:

1. **Integrations:** Integrate Canva with other tools and platforms (e.g., Google Drive, Dropbox) to streamline file management and collaboration.

2. **Templates and Brand Kits:** Create and use templates and Brand Kits to maintain consistency across designs. This speeds up the creation process and ensures brand compliance.

3. **Design Automation:** Use Canva's design automation tools to create batch designs, such as social media posts

or promotional materials, efficiently.

4. **Mobile Accessibility:** Access Canva on mobile devices to work on designs anytime, anywhere. The mobile app allows for on-the-go editing and collaboration.

5. **Training and Support:** Utilize Canva's resources, tutorials, and customer support to learn new features and troubleshoot issues, enhancing overall workflow efficiency.

Example Project: Collaborating on a Marketing Campaign

Let's collaborate on a marketing campaign using Canva:

1. **Create a Team:** Start by creating a team in Canva for the marketing campaign. Invite team members including designers, marketers, and content creators.

2. **Design Iteration:** Collaborate in real-time on campaign materials such as social media graphics, email newsletters, and posters. Use Canva's commenting feature to provide feedback and iterate designs.

3. **Sharing and Feedback:** Share campaign designs securely with stakeholders using Canva's link sharing options. Control access permissions and gather feedback using comments.

4. **Version Control:** Use Canva's version history to track changes and revert to previous versions if needed. Maintain a clear record of design iterations.

5. **Final Approval and Distribution:** Once designs are finalized, securely share approved campaign materials with the broader team or external partners. Monitor performance and adjust as necessary.

By leveraging Canva's collaboration features and optimizing workflow productivity, teams can effectively manage design projects and achieve impactful results. In the next chapter, we will explore advanced tips and tricks for maximizing creativity and efficiency in Canva. Let's continue this creative journey and unlock even more possibilities with Canva!

Chapter 15: Advanced Tips and Tricks in Canva

In this final chapter, we will delve into advanced tips and tricks to maximize creativity and efficiency in Canva. These techniques will help you unlock new possibilities and elevate your design projects to the next level.

Advanced Design Techniques

1. **Mastering Canva Pro Features:** Explore advanced features available with Canva Pro, such as Magic Resize, Brand Kit, and unlimited storage. These features enhance productivity and customization options.

2. **Using Custom Fonts:** Upload and use custom fonts in your designs to maintain brand consistency and stand out from pre-existing templates.

3. **Creating Custom Templates:** Design and save custom templates tailored to your specific needs and brand guidelines. This saves time and ensures consistency across projects.

4. **Exploring Effects and Filters:** Experiment with a variety of effects and filters to add depth and creativity to your designs. Adjust opacity, blur, and color effects to achieve desired visual impact.

5. **Utilizing Design Grids and Alignment Tools:** Use design grids and alignment tools to create balanced and professional-looking layouts. Ensure elements are evenly spaced and aligned for a polished finish.

Maximizing Productivity

1. **Keyboard Shortcuts:** Learn and utilize keyboard shortcuts to navigate Canva quickly and perform common tasks efficiently. This speeds up workflow and enhances productivity.

2. **Batch Editing:** Use Canva's batch editing feature to apply changes to multiple designs simultaneously. This is useful for updating designs with new branding or seasonal themes.

3. **Collaborative Design Boards:** Create collaborative design boards to gather inspiration, share ideas, and collect feedback from team members or clients. This fosters creativity and collaboration.

4. **Exporting Options:** Explore various exporting options in Canva, such as PDF, PNG, or JPEG formats. Choose the appropriate format based on the intended use of your designs.

5. **Learning Resources:** Take advantage of Canva's extensive library of tutorials, courses, and design resources. Continuously learning new techniques and staying updated with industry trends enhances your design skills.

Example Project: Designing an Interactive Presentation

Let's design an interactive presentation using advanced techniques in Canva:

1. **Choose an Interactive Template:** From the Canva dashboard, select "Presentation" and choose an interactive template.

2. **Customize Interactivity:** Add interactive elements such as clickable buttons, links to external content, embedded videos, and animated transitions.

3. **Integrate Data Visualization:** Use Canva's charts and graphs to visualize data within your presentation slides. Customize colors and styles to match your branding.

4. **Engaging Multimedia:** Incorporate multimedia elements like audio clips or GIFs to enhance engagement and convey information effectively.

5. **Review and Test:** Preview your interactive presentation to ensure all elements function smoothly. Test interactivity and usability across different devices and screen sizes.

By applying these advanced tips and tricks in Canva, you can elevate your design projects, streamline workflows, and create impactful visual content. Whether you're designing for marketing campaigns, presentations, or social media, Canva's versatile tools empower you to unleash your creativity and achieve professional results.

www.ingramcontent.com/pod-product-compliance
Lightning Source LLC
Chambersburg PA
CBHW040758240526
45474CB00008B/95

* 9 7 9 8 3 2 9 6 4 7 2 9 7 *